MINER
TO
MEDIUM

By Geoff Edgerton Hutchison

CON-PSY PUBLICATIONS MIDDLESEX

First Edition
2006

© Geoff Edgerton Hutchison

Published by

CON-PSY PUBLICATIONS

P.O. BOX 14,
GREENFORD,
MIDDLESEX, UB6 0UF.

ISBN 978 1 898680 42 0

INDEX

DEDICATION

I wish to dedicate this book to Nancy my wife for all the support and encouragement she has given me over the years we have been together.

Thank you Nancy.

CHAPTER 1
THE HIDDEN AGENDA

WHO IS Geoff Edgerton Hutchison? This is my journey to where I am today. I am a Medium Healer and Teacher, I was born in Scotland in Feb 1944 at a place called CATRINE in AYRSHIRE. At a very young age, my brother and I were sent to Sunday school this was Church of Scotland, we always had to have our best clothes on and change them when we got back home. From that one we moved on to the Pentecostal which was Sunday School again, but our parents weren't religious, in fact the only time I can remember them going to church was to pay their respects at Weddings Funerals and Christenings, I never thought about it before, most of my friends never went either, but it was some thing we were told to do so we did it and really we were not permitted to miss any. I suppose I must have taken a lot in as you do at a young age, but there was a lot I just could not under stand. Living in a rural area there was plenty of open fields and woods, where I played in with my friends, of course there wasn't the danger there is today. I played a lot of football for my school and the local scout team which I belonged to, but as children do at times I became ill I was still only a boy and being ill and laid up in bed for what I thought was weeks on my own, I read the Bible from cover to cover why did I read the Bible I still cant answer that to this day there was a lot I still could not under stand, why did I do it, I don't know, I also learnt to recite the books of the Bible but for what purpose. Maybe it was to help me later on with a journey that I still had to take that I knew nothing about yet. The only other times I attended church, was when I was in the army and this was for what was called church parade and if your name came up for that there was no way out. Even At this stage I never thought of becoming a Spiritualist or even heard of them, let alone being a healer and medium, that was the farthest from my thoughts. This did not start until 1991 when I was working as a mine official underground. This was at the time when the mines around were closing. I would walk around my district (this was the work area that was given to me for that shift.) It was dark with only a cap lamp to light the way for me. The ground above and around would move also the roof supports would make weird noises, but in areas where there was no one around the hair on the back of my neck would stand up. I often wondered whether it was me, or was I picking up some other feeling, or was I just frightened?

I would sit in different areas to write my report or have to pump water out from an area that was prone to water rising, I would always say a prayer, this made me feel a lot safer, and I felt that someone was listening or watching over me. The thought often crossed my mind what would my friends who worked with me think if I told them what I was thinking, or what was going through my mind. I remember one day in particular I had finished my shift at the coal face and started to walk out towards the pit bottom (this is where the mine shaft extends from the top or ground level to the area underground where it stops and roadways go off in different directions.) Well from the coalface travelling out to the main road there are no lights only the one we had on our helmets that we used to work with and guide us as we walked about, I hadn't gone 100yds when my cap lamp went out and all I was left with was my DAVEY mine safety lamp this was used to test for gas not to see where you was going, and I was on my own so I turned the wick up on my safety lamp and proceeded on my way out this was about 1-2 miles from the main road which was lit up. I must have gone about half way very slowly watching my footing when in the distance I could see one or two lights coming towards me this was the next shift coming on, but can you imagine what they must have thought at only seeing a very small light bobbing up and down about 2ft from the floor and

5

not being able to see the person carrying the lamp, it really makes you wonder what picture they had in their minds till we were able to see each other? As the pressure built up around me of losing my job and being unable to support my family, this started to have a toll on my health, just like most of us in every-day life who see the financial structure of the family unit about to be taken away from us. I started to feel tired and all the other symptoms that go with stress, the one that was troubling me, was one day as I was walking home and started to get pains in my chest, this lasted for a few days, I went to the doctors then in turn to hospital for check-ups thinking this was a heart attack. With the onset of this it put me off work for a good few weeks. So with the time I had on my hands I really wanted to get well, but finding out that the chest condition was caused by stress and not a heart attack I set about trying to relax.

At this time my wife NANCY was sitting with a group of friends going through awareness classes for self-development and working to build that link between the material world and the spiritual world, which she had been doing for some time. Nancy's background was that her MUM and DAD both were in Spiritualism for most of their lives and when they went to churches, or to visit clients to give healing, NANCY would have to go as well and most of the time played outside, but that is another story. I for my part even being married to NANCY for 26 years up till now, I still was not interested in Spiritualism, but I suppose I was like a lot of men, I didn't believe or did I and not let on, this is how we men work sometimes when there is something around that we don't understand and call it a load of rubbish, I had not felt any thing or seen any thing to draw me to search out what Spiritualism was. But I had to do something about this stress. I had read many books on meditation and its benefits, such as being able to relax and look at life from another direction, but there are many ways of doing this, as no doubt various therapists and consultants would point it out. So I had to find the way that would suit my way of life at present.

I would sit in the morning after NANCY went to work, with a nice piece of music, just loud enough that the sound trickles into my ear, this is the best way that I can indicate the level that the sound was at. I still use this to this day when I work with music, but to continue I would close my eyes and not concentrate on anything at all, but allow the pictures to pass through my mind, not concentrating on any one thing in particular, this is quite hard to do because our minds so work that it is never empty. Some meditation techniques are such that one has to try and clear ones mind, but I find that most difficult. At first I would just sit in a comfortable chair with my eyes closed and listen to the music and watch the pictures pass through my minds eye. In time I was feeling quite relaxed with this process, and as I gradually sat more often I started to get what I call faces appearing instead of the every day thoughts, it was about this time that NANCY said to me if I can get you into our group would you come and sit with us. I had still not been near a Spiritualist church at this time.

So one Sunday soon after when my wife was getting ready to go to church as she quite often did, I said to her you "don't mind if I come with you tonight" Well this was something that was never expected and I suppose this was the first bite of the cherry so to speak. I was surprised at the way the service was held, on the contrary to what was the common belief that every one held hands and all the lights were out. It was not much different in content to some of the other churches that I had attended, in that prayers were said hymns were sung and philosophy was given out (this being not much different to the sermon given in other churches) in that the talk was about love for our fellow man, and the flowers and animal kingdom created by God, but there was no trimmings it was followed by a demonstration of mediumship this was something new (this is were evidence is given that life is continuous) descriptions of someone who has passed or an illness they passed with or just in a light hearted way to say that they are still close to us. This I could understand, I was under no pressure at all it was very relaxing, unlike when I was younger and had to go to church and Sunday school because it was the thing to do, I never regretted it like now I can compare one to another.

I was soon invited to sit in circle with my wife and others; this was called a development circle and was led by a working medium, not everyone wanted to be a medium for some it was enough to develop the skills, and for others just to sit and meditate with like minded people was enough. I for myself wasn't sure in which direction I wanted to go, but was fascinated by what was happening while I sat in meditation. Our circle leader would ask us as a group to follow on a short journey that she would describe step by step. This is a process called visualisation meditation to enable us to discipline our mind and thought pattern, this would only last for about 10 minutes or 15 minutes then we would be allowed to let our minds accept whatever pictures and shapes that came to us, this lasted about the same as before, and when it was finished each in turn would describe what we had seen and what we thought it may mean.

I must explain at this point that not everybody is able to see pictures, so now you are asking how can you describe something you can't see. It took me some time to work this out also, but at first I sat there as thou my TV wasn't switched on and wondered how the others could tell us in such detail what it was that they had seen and experienced, I wonder how many of us have been in this situation, and how many still are, I will try to explain this part of awareness at a later stage. All this was put into a 1hr session per week. I would also sit at home with my wife NANCY on another night, I was Hooked I couldn't get enough!! But let me say at this stage, my preparation and meditation were always well disciplined. As I found out later they had to be.

I along with others would go once a week to our medium friend JEANNETTE'S home for our sitting and continued education, I say this because every time we got together there was always something new for us to talk about from the sitting, and of course as we were all becoming good friends what was happening in our daily lives. It wasn't long after this at one of our get togethers that JEANNETTE said to me in front of the others GEOFF, you will be working on the rostrum in 2 years time, this I didn't want at this stage, I wasn't ready I can't say I hadn't thought about it, but others who started before me surely they would be ready before me, panic was I going to be good enough to be a link to work with spirit, there was still so much I had to learn, still so much I didn't know, we were now into 1992 just over a year from me being introduced to the circle. We continued to learn how to be aware of the spirit around us also the spirit within, I can remember while sitting with others feeling the cobweb effect on my face that we all get at different stages in our development, this I put down at the early stages to the energy field changing around the body. Once you sit in an environment of relaxation and meditation the energy around the body begins to slow down this allowing the breathing to be slower and deeper, and the pulse rate to slow therefore taking the pressure away from the heart allowing the body to be in a state of relaxation in return we get the feather like touch on the face.

This is a very good exercise for those who suffer with stress. What else could happen when we first start to sit? We get fidgety in our seats and can't sit still this may happen after we have only sat for a few minutes but the more we practice the better we get until this doesn't happen, so at the beginning there is a lot to understand so that we can go forward with a sound foundation on which to build our knowledge of working with spirit. Let me make it quite clear at this stage we are not talking about auras. Which will be dealt with later.

Later we would be asked as we finished our meditation, to see if we could return to full awareness with a message, no matter how short, or something that only that person in the group could understand and accept as being passed from the spirit world to the material world through the physical link which was the sitter. YES there are many thousands of times then and as we progressed in our training, is it them or is it my mind taking over, and this doubt will keep coming up time and time again. As I continued to progress in the training that I was getting, my link with the spirit world was getting stronger, you ask how is this possible, if I put it this way, think of a drain pipe that is full of sediment from all the years of not being used and then one day someone clears out the approaches to the pipe allowing it once again to be used, the water takes some time to get through, well I feel that our bodies are used like a drain pipe the more we use the link and clear that blockage, the stronger and clear we will be able to work with the spirit world, I say spirit world because we work with more than one communicator, later it gets a bit more complicated.

We practiced giving a message to different people in the group, first of all by trying to interpret what we were being shown, in either picture form or cartoons or just shadows. With JEANNETTE'S help on what the signs or pictures could be, only what they could be, because if it didn't sound right or feel right then you went with what you were feeling. Remember it is what you feel the massage is about, and who it is for that is of importance. We continued to use various tools such as ribbons, personal items, and photographs, this was to build up our sensitivity and awareness, from the vibrations off the item that had been handled by some other person, we never knew who had held the item till we had finished Then we would see how accurate or how close we came to being correct, what must be remembered is that we were all learning and not getting it correct is frustrating, but it is how the learning process works, so all of my friends who are reading this book and want to be mediums be patient it does improve with practice.

CHAPTER 2
MY COMMITMENT

There would be two groups one on a Tuesday night and one on a Thursday, and every now and again we would get together and work, the idea was that we didn't know anything about each other, this was the start of working with strangers which may I say gets one a little nervous, and the determination to do the best you can and get it right. Everyone in the group no matter what they were sitting for all had a go, there was still plenty of work to do for me at least I still wasn't satisfied. I was now going to churches on a regular basis, not so much for a message but to watch how other mediums worked and maybe pick up some advice, I wanted to know as much as I could, I wanted to get it right, I didn't wont to stand on the rostrum and make a fool of myself and I suppose we all get like that, I kept being told trust spirit, they wont let you down, but I wanted more assurance than that, I wanted to know the whole message and keep it in my head before I stood up, but I'm sorry to say that's not how it works. For all those who have been down this path before me know what I am talking about, for those who haven't it's like working without a safety net. But it does take time to accept that, indeed what you are getting is in fact the communication that spirit wish you to pass on. The next stage of my training was to attend a night at a church with others of the group who wished to have a trial run at being a medium for the night, or few minutes!! This is called a Fledgling night, which really means trainees. We would take it in turns to stand up and give to the person in the audience whom we thought the message was for, this was sometimes only something very little, or some would give a bit more, but each of us at some stage would get stuck, by that I mean we would not understand what was being given to us so we couldn't pass on the information accurate and instead of the answer to what we were saying being yes, then came the reply no I can't take that, WHAT do I do now? At this stage again you try to put it right, if we couldn't, I know through talking to others we would say sorry I haven't got anything else for you and sit down, remember this was the first time out at a church and the nerves, well they just take over. Some others just sit there and don't get up, but just have the experience of being on the platform for the first time.

Don't think that I wasn't nervous because I was, but not as much as some, and as I look back now on my time working in the mines, one of my jobs was as a union rep and we all know what that takes, you need to be able to stand up and talk to other people from the front, I did take courses on public speaking, but before that I was a quiet person, and didn't want to get involved so even then spirit were grooming me and I didn't know it, because if I had to stand up in front of people and talk, let alone give messages, I don't think I would have done it and spirit new this, and to this day I really believe that my preparation started without me knowing.

As I progressed over the next few months working more in a workshop situation and learning to understand what the messages were that were being given, it was getting near the time for me to start putting my training into practice. But to go it alone, not yet! There had to be someone who I could work with that could help me build up the confidence, that was needed to do a full service, this is the opening prayer, the philosophy, the mediumship and the closing prayer. We had taken it in turns while in the circle to do all this but never did it as a service, in looking back I think it would have been a big help if the two groups had got together a few times and had a bit of practice. But of course there is always ways of doing it, and the tried and tested one was to go out with a medium that guided you through the steps one at a time. I can remember going out with just such a person, there we were, arrived at the church, butterflies in the stomach, when it was time to start the service the chair person asked and who is opening in prayer, very quickly I pointed to my companion, this wasn't all that strange because most fledglings who go out to work for the first time only do one part of the service. That is the part of the clairvoyance, some may only manage one communication, and others may manage two or three. Let me say that it is not because they cannot do it, but that the nerves and the butterflies make it quite difficult. Then as you progress different parts are added, with me it was the closing prayer. Never try to put into the prayer something that you have rehearsed say it straight from the heart because you will mean it, and you will give it warmth and depth, REMEMBER it is your thoughts, your feelings of love, say it as you would say your nightly prayer, you don't rehearse that.

So we are now into my training proper, you notice I still class myself, as a trainee it is unbelievable how much there is to learn, the final outcome will be reached but we must be patient and not rush, I see so many who are capable of working properly but have never completed there apprenticeship. This friends has taken me two years to reach this stage. I know with some it takes longer the first part of the prediction (on the rostrum in two years) wasn't far out.

All this time my wife Nancy was supporting me, again I must say I was and am very lucky that we both have the same interest, now it was that I started to visit churches about once a month to go on the rostrum, but still with another person and really the more mediums I could go out with the more I could work. The unfortunate thing is that not all mediums want to have a trainee with them, so myself and a friend of ours who sat in circle and was quite good at giving messages teamed up and started to get bookings in our own right I must tell you that my working partner was a girl named Yannina, and she was full of life she could work in front of group of people and they would take her to their hearts. But as time went on Yannina

14

wasn't really bothered about working to much in churches so she now does private readings and helps out in churches if she happens to be there and the speaker fails to turn up, but this is the same at most churches if at the last minute there is a hiccup the person who is in charge of the service for that night may ask for help, and like me if I was in the church I would volunteer with help but at least it would give me a bit more experience.

Now you are thinking well that's all well and good but what if that circle finishes as sometimes they do, this did happen and myself my wife and one or two others went somewhere else this was to a friend of ours but this only lasted for a short time then one left then another and another, I lasted about a year we were very good friends, but I felt that this circle wasn't right for me so I left. I have always been told if you are in circle and you feel it's not right or you are uncomfortable for what ever reason then leave it doesn't help you to progress and it won't help the circle if you stay, I know it is hard to find somewhere else if you leave but spirit will always find an opening for you again that precious word be patient. But I do sincerely believe that if it doesn't feel right then move on.

I believe that I must continually practice, train, call it what you will, to be a good link for spirit, and there are so many ways to do this you can only be as good as the effort you put in, and for me it must be 100%. Very early on when I first started to work for spirit and with spirit I made a commitment. I gave my life to God the GREAT SPIRIT. Why? I hear you ask, I felt that at this time it was something that I had to do, there seemed to be a little voice inside me urging me on this is my commitment which may not be for others.

Let me hastily say I still live the earthly life that I came hear for I still make mistakes, on the contrary to what my wife NANCY sometimes says, and yes I enjoy a drink, but only in moderation, I would like more money, never be frightened to say what you have done, or what you want out of this life, believe in yourself and most things are possible. Believing in ones self opens many doors none more so than allowing spirit to work through you and with you.

I still strive to get it right I want to be better than I am now and to that end I still attend different courses that are run, I am not in competition with anyone, but I push myself and by doing so I push my spirit friends, my Guides and helpers, to work just as hard and we work well as a team.

I will now try to explain a little about how a medium works. You have probably heard the words clairvoyance, clairsentience, and clairaudience, no matter I will try to explain a little about each, but first let me say that every medium works in a different way. It is important that you learn about oneself, I believe this starts when you sit to meditate not necessarily when you join a circle, sit and listen to your body, believe it or not it does talk to you, if you think of times when you start to feel ill the information you give to the doctor, such as I feel this, I feel that, you are listening to your body, and you are transferring what you are feeling into words, this is just the same when you work with spirit as I do this never changes. What does change is how you pass the information over, because no two people will interpret what they feel the same way. I could if you was confused in what you were feeling, help by suggesting various alternatives, but I must hasten to say that if none of them feel right with you, and what you think and feel you are happy with, then stay with that, this is sensing and the more you attune yourself to your body the better you are at describing what is happening. This is called clairsentience and most mediums work in this way.

The next I have chosen is clairvoyance (translated is clear seeing) this is the ability to see spirit but unfortunately not all mediums do. There are two ways of this happening the first is OBJECTIVELY which means you can see them as clear as if I was looking at you, I have yet to have that happen to me if and when it does guess who will be first through the door, joking though it is a bit daunting at the thought, if it has never happened to you before I suppose that at some stage in our development we all think this, and wonder what would happen, I am no longer afraid because I have overcome that fear. The other way and the way I see spirit is SUBJECTIVELY, this is in my minds eye, remember earlier I talked about my mind being a TV screen with a scene being played out in front of you or maybe a figure standing there for you to describe to the recipient, well that is a bit of how it works, and thirdly.

CLAIRAUDIENCE this is where you here spirit talking to you but again there are two ways for this. OBJECTIVELY which is outside the ear just as though some one was physically talking to you, or SUBJECTIVELY which is by inner ear or mind thought, and this one is the hardest because we always ask the question, is it them or me and this is where we come back to listening to your body. So as you can see it does and is quite involved.

There are always times when something happens and you put it down to spirit, like one time my wife and I were in bed and there was a light on the wall in the bedroom, this would be in the early hours of the morning and our first thought was spirit have come to visit, well we lay there watching this light for some time and after a short time our eyes started to play tricks but eventually it turned out to be the light from the moon and the movement was the clouds passing over, we were desperate to see something. But then on another night there was a pulsating light on the skirting board it would get larger then smaller it would move along the skirting then totally disappear, this was definitely spirit, we made sure that there was no light showing in from anywhere, this was wonderful we were now beginning to get proof for ourselves. This continued on and off for some time, over the next few weeks.

I continued to work in different churches and centres

around the Midlands meeting new friends in all walks of life which sometimes surprised me just who were interested in Spiritualism. But I also found that there are no boundaries. I was now working on my own and being able to give very good proof of survival, both past and present, I know some of the thinking in certain areas suggest that mediums should only give proof of survival, being related to the past and memories that could only be given by those who have taken there transition. I also believe that proof, is also in the communication, whether our friends in spirit talk of the past, or what is happening in our lives at that moment, if they talk of what is happening now, then is it not wonderful to know that they are still around us and they are still looking after us in there way.

I have witnessed the pleasure that some have had in some of the communications that have come from spirit; I have also witnessed the work of spirit in helping others along the way. One of these occasions was when a client of mine phoned me for a private reading, the client was expecting her second child and was about six months pregnant, this lady was frightened to go to hospital to have this baby because of a situation with the first, spirit had told her the gender of the baby, they had also indicated that she would not have the baby in hospital, this pleased her because she wanted to have it at home, so as time went on and the day got closer things weren't going right, the baby was turned the wrong way and the midwife was pressing for this lady to go into hospital, I was called again to ask spirit for their help, and once again they confirmed that the baby would turn and it would be born at home, but time was passing and the midwife was getting more and more concerned, I received another phone call to visit this lady who had now become a very good friend, when I arrived and we sat down I was told that the baby had turned on it's own, what good news! Then I was told that she had been given a date that if things weren't going right by a certain date about three weeks away then she would be taken into hospital this again wasn't what she wanted, so we sat and spirit confirmed that everything would be OK and I left. About a fortnight latter I received another phone call this lady was getting really worried she was having pressure put on her to go into hospital in case anything went wrong, every one was doing there job in the proper manor. She was told that if nothing changed they would take her into hospital on the Monday, I was asked if I was sure what I was being told by spirit was right, my answer was yes, but I also pointed out that we all have free will, and that if she thought that hospital was where she should be then the decision was hers. Through talking to her over the phone it was confirmed that everything would be fine and very soon so I left it at that. A few days latter the phone rang again I had no idea who it was and the voice on the other end said, GEOFF I have had my baby it was a boy and I had him at home, I had no trouble at all everything is fine and we are all very happy and by the way, the baby arrived on the FRIDAY. I think this is a wonderful example of how our spirit friends work knowing that this lady was frightened to go to hospital she eventually got her wish to have her baby at home. I continued to work as a medium, bringing the proof that our loved ones from the other side of the veil when asked do help us if and when they can.

CHAPTER 3
THE HEALER

But I was also interested in healing this being hands on. There are many ways of working as a healer you may work by putting your hands on the person in particular, or as I do work just about two or three inches away from the body, the results can be the same, again this depends on who is teaching you, of course there are rules to work by if you intend doing it properly. These are codes of conduct these are two fold, one they protect you and two they protect the client, I don't like to call them patients because I am not a doctor, and again some become good friends, all I will say is as you work always be truthful never say that you will cure the illness this is not in your hands. In modern day Society more and more people are turning to other forms of healing for a variety of reasons, spiritual healing not only helps the physical body but also helps to calm the mind.

As a healer like many others I work in a calm and stress free surroundings this enables the client to relax, it is no good trying to work in an area that is full of noise and distraction, because part of the healing process is to relax and get rid of that tension and allow the body to start to heal its self. What I never do is give the client a message when I am finished, I personally think this is wrong, if I am working as a healer then my body is being used as a channel for that healing energy to pass through me to the recipient, if I clog it up by using the channel for something else then I am not working to the best of my ability, and as a healer I will not give anything less. I mentioned earlier that discipline is very important as a medium, well it is just as important as a healer. Some say that you can't do both, but I do, I balance it out, but don't mix the two while working, work the best you can in honesty and in truth. There are many teachers out there who will show you how to become a healer, BUT will not make you a healer, this is a commitment that you undertake, so for all those who are contemplating taking this path good luck, you may find more failures than successes and it will disillusion you, remember that you are only the channel for spirit, and when there are successes how wonderful they are, the range is vast and it may take some time. Again practice and work will get you there, always be thankful for the gift you have been given and never abuse it.

I will tell you about a particular friend of mine, some time back she started with tinnitus this was confirmed by the doctor, she suffered this for some time till one day I was asked if I could help, I explained what I would do as a healer and the way that spirit work through me, I also explained that there was no guarantee that it would be removed all together. She would sit with me two or three times a week, my period of working lasts anywhere from half an hour to three quarters of an hour, this is the length of time that spirit normally work through me depending on the illness, later the sittings were not as regular but at least once a week or twice, gradually things started to change, and my friend started to find some relief from the continual ringing that she told me that she would get. This is not a short-term process it requires commitment from the healer and also the client, they must want to be well. This continued and gradual progress was made and her visits got further apart until it must have been over a two year period the tinnitus has almost gone, I say almost because she no longer has it on a regular basis it only seams to return when she gets upset, so now when that happens she sits in the quiet and relaxes which helps, so over the next few days she gets back to (normal). Look at it in anyway that you want this lady was not on tablets or medication, I can only find one conclusion that spirit once again stepped in to help her and of course my friend wanted to get well!!

There is also the time when our pet cat was injured; she

is a lovely ginger and white small cat. What happened was she was out during the day the way she normally is just popping in for something to eat as they do, but as the day had gone on we hadn't seen her this was very unusual not seeing her all day, well we rattled the dish which normally brings her but she never showed then that feeling started to creep in is she lying somewhere injured or something worse, we looked everywhere then the feeling came back, look in the shed again so this we did and sure enough, there she was rolled up in a ball in the corner. When I looked at her I could only just see her face but it looked as though one side had been totally taken away we lifted her out and sure enough all one side was black with dried blood, as we carried her into the house she was in a poor way, I cleaned the small face and it looked as though she had lost her eye or would have to loose it, the next job was to take here to the vet. But while my wife NANCY was getting things ready I sat and started to give our PENNY (the cat) some healing as I sat there I asked ALL my spirit friends to come close I asked GOD to take a hand in helping this precious little friend. What I asked for was precise, I asked that PENNY'S eye be saved even thought she may not be able to see through it and when it healed, her little face would look normal.

The vet agreed to leave the eye for a few days but repaired the damage round it and said that if things didn't change in the next few days it was possible that the eye would have to be removed. I continued to give healing three to four times a day for a long time. The out come is that our PENNY has two eyes one good the other is still there I like to think that in that one her vision is limited even if only being a blur. She has fully recovered in her self and hasn't stopped her doing what all cats do, but the one thing she did learn was that if she is unwell GO AND GET SOME HEALING, once again I believe the power of prayer and healing has been proved successful. There are many stories where the power of healing has helped, and I wish to continue working as a healer and doing good as long as I am permitted, be truthful and honest with yourself when working with the healing angles.

Remember also that being a good listener is working with the healing process, because not all illness is of the body some are created by the mind. Have I had healing, yes many times, there is one church that I go to when I am not working this is called PINEWOODS in the grounds of NEWSTEAD ABBEY a wonderful healing church, and in it's day has seen many wonderful things happen, which involved psychic surgery, but I must say this was before I started to go, but just to go to the front of the church and sit and let the healers do their work you leave with a feeling of well being, and is this not the corner stone of good health. Let me explain psychic surgery, it is when the medium/ healer over many years has worked with the doctors in the spirit world blending so close that it's like giving permission to the best surgeons to work through them, this does not happen to all, they can operate on humans and pets, without making a cut on the body, but only leave a red mark where the incision was theoretically made, and remove what ails the patient, I must hasten to add that all healers don't do this and these psychic surgeons are honest in what they do so you must check them out before ever thinking of having healing in this way.

I would like to point out at this stage that all mediums are not well paid, for the most who work round the churches all the payment that is received is travelling expenses the work is done because they want to do it, for some the travelling involved is considerable. This is to take the service on a particular night for an hour and a half or two hours (DEDICATION) that's what it's about. Of course there are private sittings where people get a great deal of comfort from the messages they receive and also the knowledge that it is in private. Not every one wants to go into a Spiritualist church, for some that is a step to far but that is not to say that they don't believe there is something else or some other force at work.

Have you noticed how much is covered on TV about the supernatural how people are intrigued by the whole mystery around it, the debates, all this helps the public to be aware of what we are talking about, that life is continuous.

As I have said before that as a medium I am always learning and so it is that I moved to the next stage along with my wife NANCY.

CHAPTER 4
NEW DIRECTIONS

Over the years that I have been working as a medium, NANCY and I have visited STANSTED HALL (the teaching college for various aspects of Spiritualism) meeting old and new friends each time we went, and each time picking up more knowledge and expanding on what we already knew. We had talked at various times about setting up a development circle, remembering when we first started, it was hard to get the knowledge that we required and the answers to some of our questions that we had, because at times our answers seemed to be just a little bit of the mark. The sense of feeling frustrated, we wanted to help others in this situation, and this was the start of our teaching program. There was no shortage of people who wanted to come and sit in circle with us, we arranged to make our night a Wednesday and start at 7 30pm, so the first part was to learn to relax, and how to meditate. I must hasten to add this was not spiritual meditation not yet, our students had to learn how to be relaxed and go through the process that I went through as explained earlier, about the fidgeting and getting comfortable, finding that calm within, we would use music to help to reduce the energy activity that was around us and allow our physical being to relax. It is a well known fact that by meditation you slow the heart and pulse rate down, and this helps to reduce tension and stress, remember you can do this with your eyes open or closed which ever you wish at this time. For the next stage we would ask our group to close there eyes and follow a short visualised meditation this is where you try to follow some simple instructions of a short journey this is to help with your mind discipline.

Try this and see how far you get don't worry if your mind wanders just bring it back to what you should be doing. First of all take the phone off the hook, then find somewhere to sit I suggest a chair with arms so if you fall asleep you wouldn't fall off, or on the floor, make sure the room is comfortably warm, find a piece of music that you like some thing that will help you to relax, don't have it to loud! (Some people can meditate without music) this is left with you to decide.

MEDITATION

Visualise a nice green field, the sun is out and the birds are singing, you are looking over the fence, in the field there is a hot air balloon, the balloon is of whatever colour you wish there is a man standing beside the basket of the balloon, he beckons you over, as you enter the field and walk across the grass the sun is hot on your back, you have a feeling of well being. You are invited to go for a ride, and you climb into the basket. You let go the rope that is holding the Balloon down on the ground and start to rise slowly, you are now above the trees, you rise a little more and you can see the country side stretching out around you, there is no sound and as you look down you can see the river winding it's way through the fields follow the river for a short time and remember what you see, when you are ready to return bring the balloon and yourself back into the field where you set off from, thank the man for the journey, be aware of the surroundings of the room that you are in and open your eyes.

If you do not see these images on your mind screen, which is just above your nose and between your eyes, don't worry still follow it through, the more you relax and try it the more you will be able to visualise each time, REMEMBER DON'T MAKE IT COMPLICATED KEEP IT SIMPLE.

When you have been sitting, and are comfortable with your meditation start to notice what is happening with your own body when you are in this relaxed state, it may get that floating feeling, or being heavy, notice your breathing it should be slowing down. Always make notes then latter on you can look back and see how you have progressed, I must admit that when I first started I couldn't see the sense in it, but believe me it is good to have a memory of events on paper.

Being able to work reading stones, jewellry, photographs, ribbons, that have been held by some one else and passed to you is a good way of learning how to work with some one else's vibration this is working Psychically, or if you prefer working within some one's AURA.

Over the time that I have been working as a medium I have also had to hold down a full time job. When I was looking for employment, after leaving the mines, I asked spirit to help me find a job that would allow me to continue doing my church work and let me continue sitting in circle each week without missing any, I was asking for a day job, but I wanted a supervisors position, not so easy to get, but after a short period of time I was given the position that I had asked for, I would finish work at 5 30pm, drive home have a light meal and be out to sit in circle at 7pm.

I would go through the same routine whenever I had a church service in the week, this lasted for 2 years and once again the job I was in was surplus to requirements, once again I was looking for a position with the same job description, and with this in mind I sat down and meditated and asked the spirit world to help me in finding a vacancy, and again in a few months I was back at work earning a living to pay our bills.

My work for spirit was getting more and more, along with church work I was involved in running a circle at our local church, which started off quite promising and progressed well but unfortunately due to the commitments that some of the sitters had in the world outside our numbers got smaller so my wife and I decided to move the group to our house and run a home circle, this became very successful as a group we blended just right, our sitters were eager to learn it was run as a workshop, every one having a go and learning from the experiences of each

27

other and themselves, we were fortunate as well that the churches around would allow them to have a go in front of there congregation. I must say that if you asked some of them today if they ever thought that they would progress as far as they have the answer would be no, and to be honest they have worked very hard BUT like the rest of us there is still a long way to go.

With working for spirit I was beginning to get more and more proof of the continuous world through readings given to other people and communications being verified as accurate, some within a very short time of the passing of a loved one.

My progress was beginning to take a different path, as I was sitting in circle I was becoming aware that something else was taking place, I seemed to be drifting deeper in my meditations, and feeling the affects of over shadowing, this is where spirit in my opinion draw close and work on the face with feather like touches, with me sometimes I would feel my nose flatter, larger or I my feel I have a moustache, some of the sitters who are with me can see different faces appear in front of mine, but my face seems to be blanked out allowing only the face from the spirit world to be seen, some mediums who sit for physical phenomena go through a very disciplined and strict program, but at the stage I was at this wasn't really necessary, but that's not to say it was done haphazardly, the rules of sitting in circle still are as important. We would sit for about 30 minutes allowing them to take turns at showing themselves we would use a light but not a Red one as some do; we used a small clear lamp placed in the corner of the room. This was to try and eliminate the question of shadows being cast and doubt as to whether it was the lamp or not. The feedback from the other sitters was wonderful to here and the descriptions of who they had seen, but for me the feelings I received as each one took their turn was over whelming love and emotion, I can remember one time the tears streaming down my face but not of sadness, but of joy of being able to come and have a look around, I never felt anger at all at any stage from our friends who came to visit, I am privileged and honoured to be the channel they have chosen to work through at this time.

As an ordinary man looking back, I never in my wildest dreams thought that I would one day be a Spiritualist or a medium, and doing the things that I am occupied with now and enjoy every minute, life and outlook took a new meaning when I stepped onto this path, my thoughts of what lies beyond has changed so much and yet I still search for more and more evidence but with a difference, I feel a lot more at peace with myself than I have done at any other time in my life before. This is not to say I still don't have good days or bad days because I do, this is life, but I look at them differently.

As we continued to sit our circle had come to a major point in our development, that is a decision had to be made, those who were happy just to sit and not go any further with there development were sadly asked to leave so as the others could advance that bit further in preparing to work on the platform, once this part was completed our friends had the knowledge and the belief that spirit would not let them down, it was now up to them to go out and work privately or around the churches the decision was their's this is the free will we all have. Although that was the end of that group, our circle continued but in a different format.

As I said before my wife and I have always looked at going that bit further and seeking more knowledge about working with spirit, and so it was that we started a TRANCE CIRCLE this was a continuation really from what was happening before, I had talked about the over shadowing but we continued to go forward, we had already had some success previously with different spirit friends joining us. One of the very first was a CARDINAL THOMAS who for a very long time would help me with my philosophy and to be honest he may still be with me, at times when I was in TRANCE he would come and talk to the others and answer questions, some information that he gave was that he was in YORK in the early 18th century he described the job of administering to the soles outside the wall's as well as within the walls but he was not or did not seem to be part of the CATHEDRIAL, and this got every one a bit baffled, so one sunny day 4 of us decided to go to YORK to follow up on the clues that CARDINAL THOMAS had given us. We called at various churches looked at some records inside the walls but mainly out as was indicated.

Yes we found one or two and tried to put the jigsaw together but there seemed to be the bit missing that would pinpoint the gentleman to a specific church or area I would like to think that we did find the proof but in our eagerness and running around we missed vital clues and sadly we have not been back to try again but that did not stop us getting some lovely messages and guidance from him. At about the same time or maybe a little later another communicator was very much drawn to our group his name was CHARLES, that is all he wanted to be known as, but what he did describe was that he owned a big house in the south of ENGLAND he spoke with an upper class accent and was very happy to take his dog out and walk around his land this got him away from the family, a very pleasant man would talk for some time to the group on his life style and how it had changed but still preferred his laid back way of looking at life in his ageing years.

Little did we realise that all was going so well, no one took notes or recorded any of these sittings and how many times has this happened and the advice that we give to all those who sit with us, keep a record then you can look back and see how far you have come, unfortunately for these at the beginning, all we have are the memories and the lesson not to do it again, keep a record.

There was also one more that I will tell you about, and

this gentleman never spoke at any time not until months later when he again while I was in trance told the group what his job was with our group and also with others that he visited, and that was to make every one laugh. At various times maybe because the group was a little low or for what ever reason this gentleman would come and all he would do was at first just sit and grin and the smile got bigger and bigger then laugh, well the first time this happened my wife NANCY got really afraid and wondered what on earth had we got here and it frightened her, but he did make everyone laugh, after the first time and the group knew what was happening they eagerly awaited his return the laughter was so warm and genuinely uplifting everyone joined in you just couldn't help it. Yes you can say he was like a jester, can you think of a better way of uplifting the vibrations than this? Spirit just know what we need and always come up with the goods in the most unusual way, then it would be back down to the work of blending and jelling with the spirit world and allowing the experiment to take it's course.

Remember that all the work that is done with spirit is an experiment it may not turn out the way you thought it might but it is a working together to bring the proof that our friends and loved ones continue on in another life, which we only get a glimpse of, and isn't it heart warming to know they still look after us in there way. We still sit and enjoy the company of those from spirit but not as much as we would like, but I know that it will build up again when the time is right, as for now there are a few changes going on and we must all be patient.

I know that as each of us work with our spirit friends there are times when we want to experiment more and more, well one of the times while sitting we decided to try and get a build up of energy to move the table we were sat round, we tried this for a couple of weeks and nothing happened but we continued only for a short time at each sitting, then one night as we sat we could here this sound just like a train starting to get faster and faster, then we could smell what I can only explain as someone using a sanding machine, a very strong smell of wood, this was so real that my heart was really pounding with excitement, unfortunately the table did not lift but this was something new and it caused a lot discussion around the group as to just what had happened. But true to form as I was told some time ago you don't mix development with psychical, because there were some in the group who just didn't want to be involved in it when things started to happen, and that gathering broke up, this was sometime before NANCY and I started our own training groups, now we run separate circles and both are doing well.

CHAPTER 5
SO MANY GIFTS

In November 1998 I started to suffer quite badly with arthritis in my feet and hands which so far as doing physical work was concerned took me out of the work market, but I still needed to pursue my spiritual work so for a year I worked very hard doing workshops demonstrations teaching and my church work also private readings, a lot was done for charity. I really didn't say no to any invitation to work, but come November 1999 I started to get a bit worse and in February I was taken to hospital I had lost 2st, lost all my muscle strength in my legs and arms which meant I couldn't walk, get out of bed, or a chair, had to be helped everywhere. I thought well this a fine thanks for all the work I have been doing, but as I lay in hospital for the next couple of weeks while they tried to find out what had happened by doing all the tests and still came up with nothing, I thought of my work and I can say even to this day I would never stop this gives me so much pleasure knowing that I help others in this world as well as the next. As I checked my diary for that particular time thinking I might have to cancel some bookings I was quite surprised to find that I had little or no commitments, remember that these bookings and commitments were entered in the year before. I fill my calender a year in advance, so what was it that I had missed or was spirit trying to tell me something that I had ignored?

On leaving hospital I continued to fight to walk thought I had to use the crutches I managed to get around, I am not going to bore you with the details of my illness but to say that I spent some time looking at my life up to that point, and realised that things were going to change physically and mentally. I carried on with my church work, resting up during the day so as I would have the strength to work at night, you may say that I was a little bit mad but I believe this kept me going I was doing something worth while.

My wife NANCY has always supported me in everything that I have done and from being severely restricted in my movements she had become my strength and driving force in positive thinking, (YOU WILL GET BETTER). Doing that little bit more each day and giving healing, what a wonderful gift that is to share with some one, but I never lost that purpose of why I was on this earth, to share life's worst kept secret LIFE IS ETERNAL.

Sadly though our teaching and group work had to stop but we continued to meditate together and keep our links with the spirit world open. But life does have its bright side, through this illness I have obtained a computer and a bit more spare time, I have often thought about putting a book together but like every one else never got round to it, now there are no more excuses so this is the out come, again something a few years ago I would never thought possible, isn't it wonderful how life takes it's little turns and we don't know what is round the corner.

I think I have learnt a very good lesson for this part of my life, and that is not to over stretch myself in my eagerness to work with spirit but to spread it out, I hope that for the readers who contemplate taking up this work that in there eagerness they will not be over stretched. Spirit will work with you the best way they can but I feel that we must search for the way that is best for us as individuals there are many options open to us, the use of colour, drawings, writing in its many forms, the list is endless, but what we must search for is, where is the inspiration coming from, is it from the spirit world or are we inspired from within to work in this way, it may be a combination of both, I really don't know.

If we look at poetry although I have said many times in the past the only thing I know about it is what I was taught at school and that wasn't a lot because as a young boy in

SCOTLAND that was never right, Boys and Poetry didn't mix, not until I came into this movement did I ever think of putting pen to paper in this way, although I was and still am very good at putting a letter together, I have put some poems on paper and they have come to me at all different times such as out walking, maybe at that time it was my inner self finding the balance of nature, peace and harmony with my whole self, other times snippets will come when I am in the car, which ever way I don't think it matters, as long as you are happy with the result and it gives you pleasure, but please share them with others it may be the words that you put down, are just what some one else needs at that time.

There was one occasion that I know spirit were working with me Why! Because it was too early in the morning for me to think, and the words kept repeating themselves in may head so before I got dressed I put pen to paper not knowing what the out come was going to be. But I had that feeling that this was something that they wanted me to record, or again was it a message for me in my time of need, a time where I needed that support that comfort that moment when as we all do, have doubts about where my path was taking me and the loss of a very good friend, the words went like this

LOVE

L--- is for the loneliness when our loved ones take there leave
To that bright tomorrow away from all that grief,

O---is for the opportunities that could have been,
The good the bad, the happy the sad, but with passing time all but a dream.

V----is for the very best we wish them on their way,
And as the days and years go by,
We know they will return to us one day.

E---is ever lasting the love we have for you,
Your grown up ways, your childish ways,
The little ways that are you.

LOVE---in all its glory means so much to me and you,
The pain in my heart, when we had to part,
Makes me pleased that I met you.

Yes there was a message for me, just as there will be a message in it for any one who reads these wonderful lines God bless you all.

Do not be frightened to try what ever form of communication that you think that you are drawn to, this is the way I feel that you can find out what is right for you. Just recently I have started to do some Psychic art. For those who don't know what this is I have a pencil and paper, I haven't moved on to colour yet. I sit for a few moments and meditate and get my link with spirit, now I have tried this in three different ways, I would sit in my car out side the church and as I said link with spirit and ask for a communicator to come close when this happens I draw that persons face and then ask for one or two bits of information to add to the drawn, then when I go into take the service I take the drawing with me, and sure enough in that church there is one person that this drawing is for along with the message. I have also tried sitting at home and doing the same thing before leaving and asking where they will be sitting in the church and been told and wrote this on the paper also that they were late coming in, these experiments work don't be afraid to try them there is so much we don't know.

I did a drawing once before a client came for a private sitting and left it on the settee I didn't know who it was or where it belonged but as the client entered the room he said

36

what are you doing with a drawing of my aunts picture, I then knew where it belonged she was his communicator that day and was with me before he arrived at least 3 hours earlier, there are various situations like this that it is just not coincidence it must be something else, but I know what it is, it is undoubtedly more proof in the jigsaw that life is continuous.

Am I an artist? No my drawings have gone from match stick men to something that can be recognised but I know they will get better with the help of our friends in the spirit world. I have often been asked by NANCY, why don't you go for art or drawing lessons, I don't think I want to do that, at present give me a pencil and paper and without linking with spirit I can not draw, if I had lessons I think there would always be a doubt how much have I put into the portrait, we are back at the same old question is it me or is it them? I suppose there are many out there that would say that being able to draw would be an advantage, it's a little like driving once you know how to do it you cut corners, if you don't know what is the right way or wrong way but leave it to instinct or intuition then that has got to be right for you, and if you are happy with the outcome then who is to say that its wrong. I now believe very strongly that how you feel and react to situations in life are very important, but work with your whole body not just your mind.

As time has moved on I am more and more leaving my walking stick behind and I thank the medical profession for there work also the spirit world and my DARLING NANCY, for their patience and perseverance in getting me back to a good positive out look and strong body, never give in to negative situations that are around but look how they can be changed to positive ones. The balance that we create in our lives is what takes us step by step through that plan that is laid out for us and it is up to us as individuals to make it work the best way we can, each one will approach it in different ways, but for each one, it will be right for them, life is hard but who said it was going to be easy? As long as from each mistake that is made we are able to learn something and move on.

The North American Indians have a saying," we have only borrowed this earth". So let us use it wisely and treat it with respect and hopefully one-day man will come to his senses. To abuse a child is a crime, to abuse the earth is just as bad but we still have to come to terms with this, but sadly this still seams a long way off, as we become more aware, and spiritual, maybe the seeds have been sown for future generations.

I believe there are many like me who through there lives go from day to day really not aware of what potential there is within themselves until one day for whatever reason we have suddenly got some thing and don't know what to do with it, then the search is on to find out as much as possible, because when you are 50yrs and over there doesn't seem to be enough time left to complete this new mission that we have embarked on.

Believe me friends, I said earlier I started late I was 49yrs old when I started and since that time I am really enjoying myself, And to think all this is freely accessible, religion or colour does not come into it, its universal for all creeds young and old alike rich or poor we each can have a piece of it.

I said before that being a medium does not always lead to being rich in financial terms but it does make one rich in knowledge and personal growth, I now look at other people in a different light, a long time ago I worked for citizens advice and they teach you not to be judgmental which at that time I found very hard not to be, but a few years down the road I find it a lot easier,

I am not saying that I don't have thoughts, I do, but I try to keep them under control, therefore if you are conscious of let me say negative thoughts then we can control them and turn them round. I am not saying that every time this happens we must have a battle with ourselves, not at all but it is nice to know that we can do something about it.

Life must be lived to the best each of us can get out of it sometimes there are situations that just cant be shaken off, and these need to be looked at in a different light, and approached differently but asking for help through prayer and from spirit is in its self an awareness that we are not alone. The make up of what we are, is that we only ask for help when it is either to late or the last resort, isn't it sad that we turn to our spirit friends only when we are in need. While on the earth plane they gave us love and were about us not just when in need but all the time, don't you think that they would like to just communicate in a gossip kind of way as they did before, I'm sure they would. I am also sure that if we all open to that unseen force that surrounds us there will be some wonderful times and memories shared, and then we will become more aware of our own inner strengths.

Being a medium and a healer takes time as I have said before, but knowing that this is what you want to do is a step on a long road of self discovery, being able to remove the obstacles that keep appearing in front of us and going forward is the test that you have to endure, always have faith in what it is that you have undertaken, seek out the teachers that are right for you as an individual because you will come across some that you just can't jell with, these could be close friends it doesn't mean to say that you fall out with them no! It means that they are not the teachers for you at this time.

Life in this earthly condition makes one wonder just where it is that we are going, and what it is that we are here for, over a period of time I have thought about this, I have heard it said that there is a plan set out before you come to earth may be so, but that doesn't change the fact that you still have your part to play.

CHAPTER 6
AN UNLIKELY MEETING

I believe that it is up to the individual how they get through there time on this earth, if you sit back and do nothing then that's exactly what you get, if you do very little then you get a bit more than nothing, what I am saying is that the more effort that you put into living the more that you get in return. Money does not come into it, it is all about quality of life, and how each of us take the opportunities that are put in front of us, we are that busy looking for the obstacles that give us pain, that hold each of us up and hurt us, that we think we need this sort of challenge, before we can progress. Rubbish!! If you see it coming and then do something to avoid it or change your thinking then I think that that is a more important lesson than being hurt all the time. You are becoming aware of your surroundings and the options that are in front of you, but will we learn? It seems that the human race would rather stumble from one disaster to another, this is not God or the spirit world to blame this is MAN in search of something that he has already. That is the power within him to create a better under standing for himself and his world around, we are all responsible for our bit of space, our moment, and our actions. Until we each think of this in some form, I have my doubt whether things will ever change, I know that my space has changed over the years and my thinking, the difference with me is that I wanted that change DO YOU?

The spirit world do not block us in what we do or try to achieve we do, they give us assistance by giving us signs, or pointers, to help each of us in our every day life, but sadly we have lost that basic instinct that GUT FEELING, the instincts that we had as children, simple and not complicated, no hidden meaning the game that us adults play.

Part of me learning to be a medium was being able to

40

look at the symbols that the spirit workers use to communicate with me and really take them as they came and not put another interpretation there, this is part of seeing what you see and give what you get, a lesson that I don't think will ever change in this work.

As I reread the previous page it was quite obvious that my helper GRAY WOLF was having his say and I thought of leaving that page out but taking my advice to you I have left it in because I really think it needs to be said for me at least.

I must tell you about a situation that happened to me about a year a go. I was asked to take a service at a Spiritualist centre, now for some time I have said that religious denominations should get together and they are, but unfortunately not the one that I am involved with, none of the others seem to want us to join them or talk with us only to tell us that it is wrong. I thought it would be interesting to speak with a minister on his views, but up till now this has not happened, but what has happened is that I arrived at this centre and there to meet me was a minister dressed as they are with the white collar, my first thought was Oh!! Or words to that affect, I have come to the wrong place, but in fact I was in the right place and he was helping to run this centre, what a wonderful eye opener for me, what made it even more unusual was that I had to give him a message from some one in the spirit world. Now if you think about it, and picture this in your mind, this is a man of the cloth fully converse with the bible sitting in the front row my mind was racing, how do I give him this message, will he accept it, of course he will, that's why he is here, but for that moment I wondered. After all my thoughts of meeting a vicar and talking about Spiritualism with him, here was one in the hall listening to the service I thought how wonderful, that we can share this moment with no barriers. There must be many more who believe, as there are attend services, good on you, but doesn't it show you just how things turn out, it doesn't always arrive the way you expect it, this certainly didn't.

I must tell you about a couple of funny things that happened to me while I was sitting in circle and this happened early on in my training, searching for a trance group to sit with I was invited to one, let me hurriedly say that in my opinion this should never happen and I did not stay there, but we were sitting for this particular person, waiting for some one to join us from the spirit world when one of the group, to this day I don't know who, asked the sitter if there was anybody there and to my surprise the answer came back no not yet they are having a little difficulty. The next one was after sitting for a while waiting for spirit to attune to the sitter, again the question was asked, "is there anybody there", and to my surprise the sitter put his hand up and said HOW!! Well, I could have fallen off my chair, and one or two of us looked at each other, needles to say we never went back. Yes I can just imagine what you are thinking, and my thoughts were probably the same, but think of it in another way, who was really kidding who, it is a shame that there are some people who want to do this kind of mediumship that they fool themselves into thinking that it is happening and therefore try to convince others, always be aware that as mediums one is always open to being labelled as being a fraud. This part is such a wide subject that it should be approached and guided through by some one who knows what they are doing, as again I found out in the early years.

Life to me has had its ups and downs and no doubt this will go on but what we must remember is that what is happening at this moment is already in the past, and all the hurt and stress that we feel, we are carrying to the future and taking it with us, we are suffering through our own inability to let go, and by letting go we can look at a new way of thinking, and new directions which are there for each and every one of us. The spirit world help us yes that is true, but we must do our part and not sit back and think that it will all be done for us,

As we, or our friends, move to the spirit world we must go through a learning process of what it is that we have to do in our new environment, sometime it is hard for that sole at this stage to take everything in, so it is like going back to school yes there is someone assigned to be with that sole to comfort them and guide them in most cases it is a loved one or a very close friend they are never alone, the bond of love is very strong in fact overwhelming, but so wonderful. Just as we feel the loss, our friends who move to the higher side feel that loss, but once it is understood that we can communicate both from the world of spirit, and us on our part from the material world, then the hurt and the pain moves to one side, forgetting those who have moved on is not an option we remember them with love and affection and so it is that our friends in the spirit world remember each one of us. The gift and privilege of working with these soles is something that I cannot put into words of one syllable.

A friend of mine passed to spirit recently and quite quickly as well, but I know that he is pulling out all the stops to get to know the system on how to communicate with us and his wife Di, as I write this part of my book I feel so warm and peace full, and I am aware of the closeness of Peter, and know that as he helped others while on the earth he will have so much work to do from the world of spirit and like all the others he will overcome the obstacles, and continue to be part of the lives of the loved ones that are left on the earth plane, we are all brothers and sisters, and there is no death, only a parting for a short time, life is continuous, don't hold on to the grudges that you had, let them all go, they are of no importance now, allow peace and love to fill your whole being and feel how wonder full it is. THIS IS LOVE FROM SPIRIT TO SPIRIT GOD BLESS YOU.

Not long after the terrible disaster of the twin towers on Sep 11th 2001 I was sitting in my living room and it was at that time of the evening that I have put aside for spirit. I went and sat in my chair and started to link with our spirit friends, I asked them to show me the situation in the world of spirit at that time, and how so many soles were cared for knowing that they would be traumatised, I was told and shown a vast amount of spirit workers joining together and taking the traumatised soles into their care there was so much love poring out to them. Believe me when I say this it was like being surrounded by light love and tenderness which comes only from the angelic beings, who's job it is to be present at any disaster no matter how large or small.

They were taken and cared for until it was time for them to meet their friends and loved ones who had already passed to the higher side of life before them, I was also told that religion or colour did not matter, they were all Gods children, and no matter whether good or bad while on the Earth, the sole was still good, we are what we are on the earth plane this is our heritage of free will which is given to us when we are born.

This disaster may have been predicted in some other books of predictions made long ago as was said in the papers, if that is the case then the spirit world was ready for so many soles in that one moment that day, but I know that with my whole being that each and every one was welcomed home to the spirit world with abounding love, no matter what their religion was, we are all the same under the one God and in time our loved ones will make their presence felt, it is Man who commits the terrible crime, and Man who must answer for his deeds. You are not judged by any one when you pass to the higher side, only that you judge your self, and look at the life you had. There is no hell only the one we create for ourselves.

My work for spirit goes on trying to find the answers that still allude me, the ones that I can under stand the ones that feel right, only you can set your goals only you can attain the standard that you want. The price is you have to work to get it and keep on working, never be satisfied, you will always find more, and astonish your self how much information that we can get from the world of spirit.

Think about it in this way, not if there is another world where our friends live, but there is another place where they have gone, and the sooner the establishment can accept this with all the proof that is available then the better we are equipped to deal with death of the physical body, and under stand what the next part of our adventure awaits us.

I hope that like me you have found your purpose and your companion on this part of your journey, if not they are both their waiting to be united with you, look to the inner self first then look around and see what needs to be changed. These are a few of my experiences on my way as a Medium and some of my thoughts as well as help from our friends on the other side, I hope they will help others who are starting out or may give some a fresh look at how they work, only YOU can decide the next part, good luck and keep an open mind, and may I share with you all the love that I have and the love that has been with me from the world of spirit while I have been writing this book, God bless all of you on your new venture in life.